Early SCIENCE Encyclopedias

LIFE SCIENCE

by Carla Mooney

Early Encyclopedias

An Imprint of Abdo Reference
abdobooks.com

abdobooks.com

Published by Abdo Reference, a division of ABDO, PO Box 398166, Minneapolis, Minnesota 55439.

Printed in China.
052024
092024

THIS BOOK CONTAINS RECYCLED MATERIALS

Editor: Arnold Ringstad
Series Designers: Candice Keimig, Joshua Olson
Production Designer: Ryan Gale

Library of Congress Control Number: 2023949537

Publisher's Cataloging-in-Publication Data

Names: Mooney, Carla, author.
Title: Life science / by Carla Mooney
Description: Minneapolis, Minnesota: Abdo Reference, 2025 | Series: Early science encyclopedias | Includes online resources and index.
Identifiers: ISBN 9781098294250 (lib. bdg.) | ISBN 9798384913528 (ebook)
Subjects: LCSH: Life sciences--Juvenile literature. | Life (Biology)--Juvenile literature. | Science--Juvenile literature. | Biology--Juvenile literature. | Encyclopedias and dictionaries--Juvenile literature.
Classification: DDC 570--dc23

CONTENTS

Giraffes are the tallest land animals on Earth.

Animals and Plants around the World

The world is full of animals and plants. They come in many shapes, sizes, and colors. They live in habitats worldwide. Life exists in cold polar regions and dry deserts. From tall giraffes to spongy mosses, Earth has amazing living things.

Studying Living Things

Life science is the study of living things. Scientists learn how animals and plants live and grow. Animals, plants, and their environments interact with each other. Together, these communities are called ecosystems. Scientists study the world's ecosystems.

Scientists called marine biologists study sea life.

There are more than 10,000 species of ants.

Millions of Species

Elephants, ants, and snakes may seem very different. But they have something in common. They are all animals. Millions of animal species live on Earth. Their appearances and behaviors differ widely. They live in many environments.

Living Things

All animals are living things. They are multicellular. This means they are made of many tiny parts called cells. Animals need food and water to live. Some animals eat plants. Some eat other animals. Animals can move from place to place. They use their senses to learn about their environments.

What Is a Cell?

Cells are the building blocks of life. Some living things are made of a single cell. Animals and plants are made of many cells.

Animals eat other living things to survive.

Spiders, such as tarantulas, are invertebrates.

Classifying Animals

Scientists classify animals by looking at similarities and differences. Animals are divided into two main groups. Animals with a backbone are vertebrates. Scientists divide vertebrates into smaller groups. These are mammals, fish, birds, reptiles, and amphibians. Animals without a backbone are invertebrates. Examples include insects, worms, spiders, and many other creatures.

Reptiles, such as snakes, are vertebrates.

FUN FACT!

About 95 percent of animal species are invertebrates.

Whales are the largest creatures on Earth.

The World of Mammals

Earth is home to more than 5,400 species of mammals. Mammals live on every continent. They are different sizes, shapes, and colors. Huge whales are mammals. Tiny mice are mammals too. Even humans are mammals.

Warm-Blooded Vertebrates

Mammals are vertebrates. Mammals are also warm-blooded. This means they can adjust their body temperatures. They can survive in hot or cold weather. This ability allows mammals to live in many climates.

Mammals such as snow leopards survive in extreme climates.

FUN FACT!

Mammals have large brains compared with other animals.

Producing Milk

Mammals produce milk to feed their young. Female mammals have mammary glands. These glands produce milk. A young mammal feeds on milk until it can eat solid food.

Many piglets can drink milk from their mother's body at the same time.

Porcupines' spiky hairs are also known as quills.

Growing Hair

Mammals grow hair or fur. A mammal's hair keeps it warm. Hair can help mammals hide. Polar bears have white fur to blend in with snow. Hair also has other special purposes. A porcupine's hair is tough and spiky. It protects the porcupine from predators.

Seals can often be seen on beaches.

Mammal Homes

Mammals live almost everywhere on Earth. Most live on land. They live on the ground, in trees, and in underground dens. Some mammals, such as seals, live on land and in the water. A few mammals live entirely in the water. They include whales, dolphins, and manatees.

Mammal Food

Mammals eat a variety of foods. Some mammals are carnivores. This means they eat other animals.

Lions, wolves, and dogs are carnivores. Other animals are herbivores. They eat only plants. Mammals that are herbivores include deer, elephants, and rabbits. Animals that eat plants and animals are omnivores. Bears and monkeys are mammals that are omnivores.

In the early stages of development, the embryos of many species look similar. This photo shows a mouse embryo.

Life Starts as an Embryo

Most mammals develop from an embryo inside their mother's body. An embryo is a fertilized egg. The growing embryo receives nutrition from the mother.

Gestation

Gestation is the time a mammal grows inside its mother. Gestation length varies by species. A female hamster carries its young for just a few weeks. Human gestation lasts about 40 weeks. Elephant mothers can carry their young for 22 months.

Live Young

Most mammals give birth to live young. Some newborn mammals, such as horses, can walk within hours after birth. Other newborn mammals need more care. Newborn rabbits are blind, hairless, and helpless. Most newborn mammals rely on their mothers for food and safety.

Marsupials

Marsupials, such as kangaroos, are mammals with a pouch. After birth, the baby crawls into its mother's pouch. It stays there until it grows enough to leave.

Newborn rabbits require care from their mother to survive.

Asian elephants can begin reproducing at about 14 years old.

Growth and Development

After birth, a young mammal grows. It learns to survive and live independently. Some mammals mature into adults quickly. Rabbits mature in a few weeks. Others, such as elephants, take years to become adults. Adult mammals can produce young.

Longest-Living Mammal

The bowhead whale is the longest-living mammal. It can live for 200 years or more.

Horse Life Cycle

Horses are usually considered adults at around the age of four.

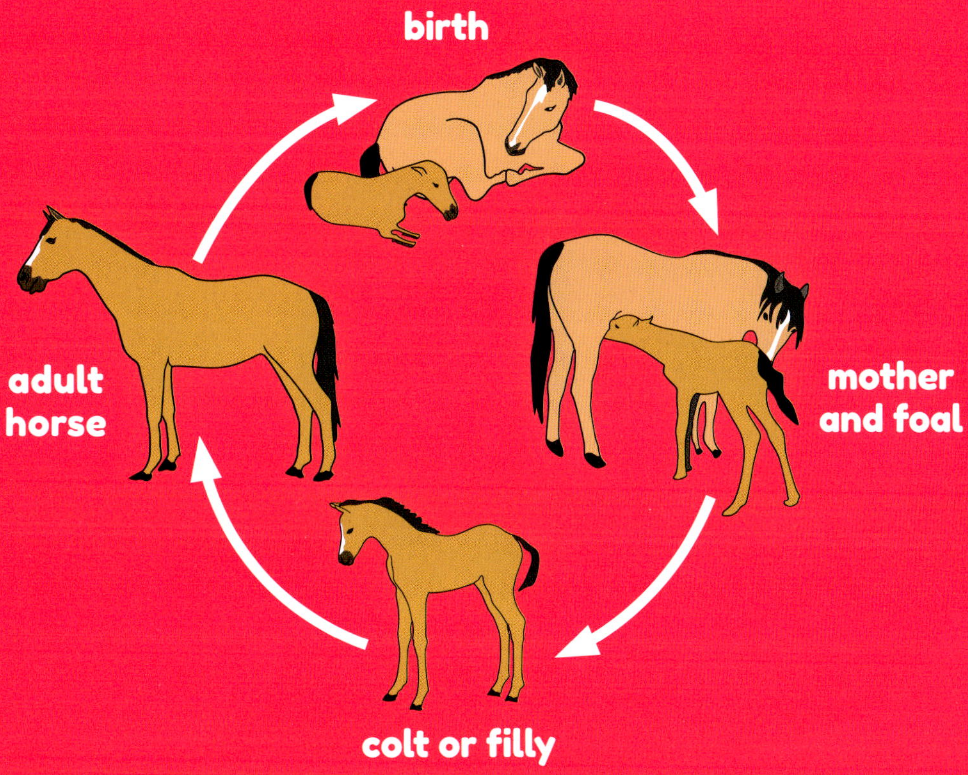

Fish Species

Fish are animals that live in the water. They come in different sizes, shapes, and colors. All fish have some things in common. They are vertebrates. Most fish are cold-blooded. Their body temperatures change depending on the temperature of the water around them.

FUN FACT!

About 32,000 fish species live on Earth.

Parts of a Fish

Many fish have the same types of fins, but the fins' shapes can differ. Some fins may be rounded, square, forked, or even heart shaped.

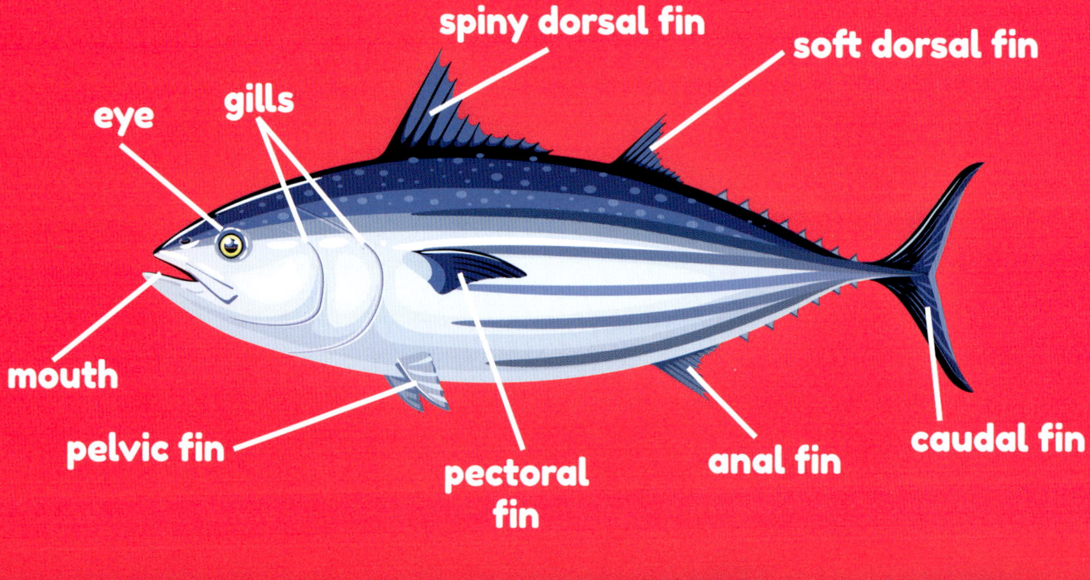

Many tropical fish are brightly colored.

Gills are typically located behind a fish's eyes.

Why Are Fish Slimy?

Fish are covered in slimy mucus. Mucus helps fish glide through the water. It makes fish slippery and harder for predators to catch.

Breathing Underwater

Fish use gills to breathe underwater. Gills are slits on a fish's head. Water runs over the gills. Oxygen in the water moves into the fish's blood. A few types of fish gulp air at the water's surface. They are called lungfish.

Moving through the Water

Fish have fins to help them swim. Their tail fins push them through the water. Fish have other fins on their backs, bellies, and sides. These fins help fish move, turn, and balance. All fish have skin. Many fish have scales that protect their skin. Fish also have swim bladders to stay afloat. These organs fill with air. They keep the fish from sinking too low or floating too high.

Crystal structures in fish scales can make some fish look shiny in the light.

Rainbow trout are found in rivers in Asia and North America.

Freshwater Fish

Fish live in almost every natural body of water on Earth. Some fish live in freshwater lakes, rivers, and ponds. Fresh water has much less salt than ocean water. Bluegills, catfish, bass, and trout are common freshwater fish.

Ocean Fish

Other fish live in salty ocean waters. Common saltwater fish are cod, flounder, tuna, and halibut. Some fish can live in both fresh water and salt water. Some fish live in deep, cold water. Other fish live in warmer, shallower water.

Fish Food

Fish eat many foods. The smallest fish eat plants, such as duckweed. Large fish eat smaller fish. Some fish also eat bugs.

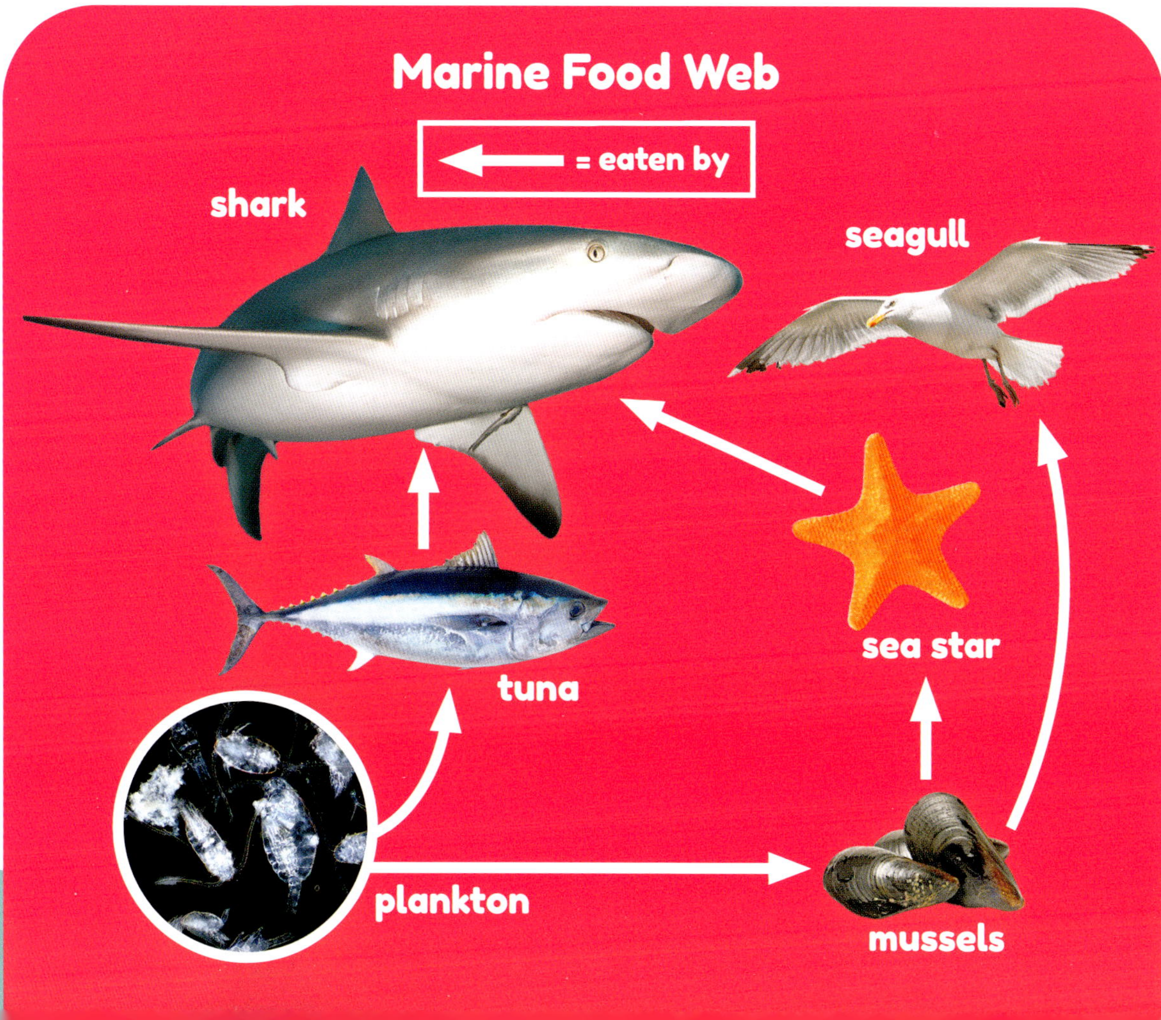

Hatching from Eggs

All fish hatch from eggs. In most species, female fish lay many eggs. Some females lay up to one million eggs at a time. Then male fish fertilize the eggs. Many eggs do not survive. Usually, only a few of them mature. Some fish eggs are fertilized and hatch in the female's body. These young are born live. Guppies and most sharks are born live.

Fish Friends

Fish may live alone or in groups. A group of fish is called a school. A school of fish swims and moves together. Some schools have hundreds of fish.

In some species, male fish guard the eggs from predators.

Fish are known as fry during their first few months of life.

From Eggs to Larvae

When the eggs hatch, they become larvae. They are still developing. Larval fish have a yolk sac attached to their bodies. They get nutrition from it. They can eat live food when their eyes and mouth fully form. They become juvenile fish.

Juvenile blue tangs are yellow. They develop a blue color as they grow into adults.

Growing Up

Young fish develop into adults in several stages. Development speed varies by species. It can take a few months to almost a year. Juvenile fish look like adult fish. But they are smaller and weaker. Predators hunt juveniles. As a result, many juvenile fish do not live long enough to become adults.

Adapt to Survive

Over time, fish species have adapted to survive. Some fish can change colors to hide from predators.

Becoming an Adult

Once a fish can reproduce, it becomes an adult. Fish with shorter life spans often become adults faster. For most fish, the life cycle begins again when female fish lay eggs in the water. This process is called spawning. Some fish spawn every year. Other fish spawn only once in their lifetimes.

Fish Life Cycle

Some fish species develop into adults in just one year. For other species this may take more than 20 years.

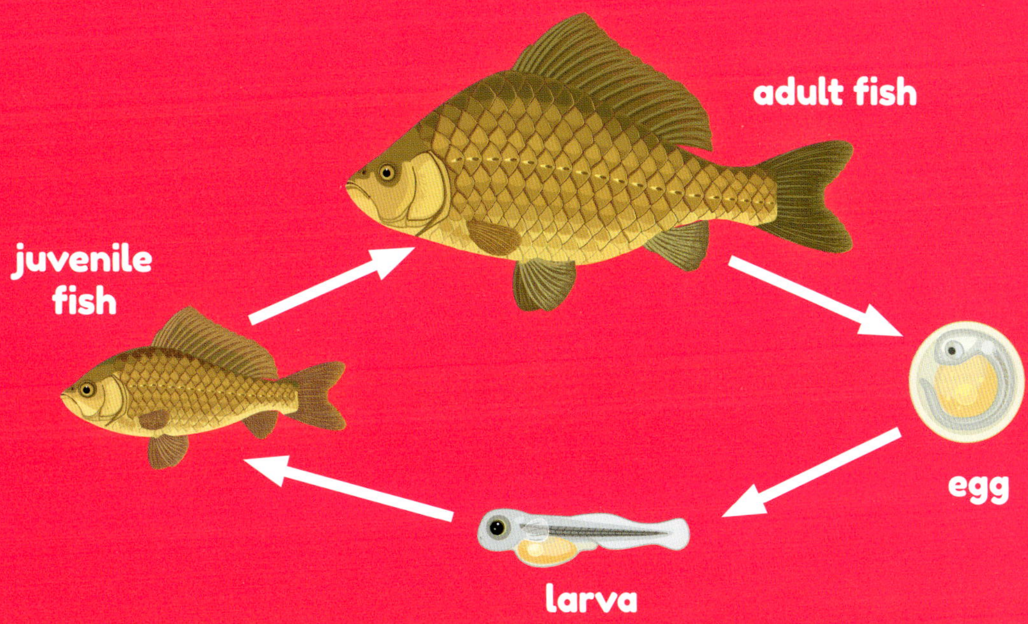

Birds usually have thin legs and lightweight bodies.

All about Birds

Birds are animals with wings and feathers. They are vertebrates. These animals are also warm-blooded.

Grounded

A few bird species do not fly. Penguins cannot fly. Instead, they use their wings to swim. Ostriches have small wings and strong legs. They walk or run instead of flying.

Flying High

Most birds are built to fly. Many of their bones are hollow. This keeps them light. Birds use powerful chest muscles to flap their wings. These wings are shaped to lift birds into the air. Air flows smoothly over the feathers as they fly. Birds use their tail feathers to steer.

FUN FACT!

Airplane wings are shaped similarly to bird wings.

Birds' wings give them amazing speed in the air.

Feathers

Birds are the only animals with feathers. Feathers help birds fly. They also protect birds' bodies. Feathers help birds stay warm or cool. They protect birds from rain.

Many Colors

Feathers come in many colors. They may help birds hide from enemies or sneak up on prey. Other feathers are brightly colored. Males may use bright feathers to attract females.

Both male and female macaws are brightly colored.

Ostriches have large feathers on their bodies but mostly bare necks.

Hummingbirds' long beaks help them reach into flowers to feed.

Bird Beaks

All birds have beaks. Birds use their beaks in many ways. Beaks let birds grab and swallow food. They help birds defend against predators. Birds also use beaks to groom their feathers and build nests.

Types of Beaks

Beaks can be many shapes and sizes. Eagles have hooked beaks to rip open prey. Sparrows have cone-shaped beaks to break open seeds. Parrots have short, curved beaks to split open hard fruits and nuts. Robins use their straight, thin beaks to catch insects.

FUN FACT!

Bird beaks contain a protein called keratin.

Bald eagles use their hooked beaks to eat small birds, mammals, and reptiles.

Some birds migrate in large V-shaped formations.

Bird Homes

Birds live in many environments. They are found in mountains, deserts, forests, and jungles. Many birds migrate from one place to another. They fly long distances for food or nesting. For example, Canada geese fly south in the winter and return north in the spring.

FUN FACT!

Birds do not have teeth. They swallow their food whole.

Bird Food

Many birds eat insects, seeds, and fruits. Some birds eat fish. Hawks and eagles eat small animals and other birds. Vultures eat dead animals.

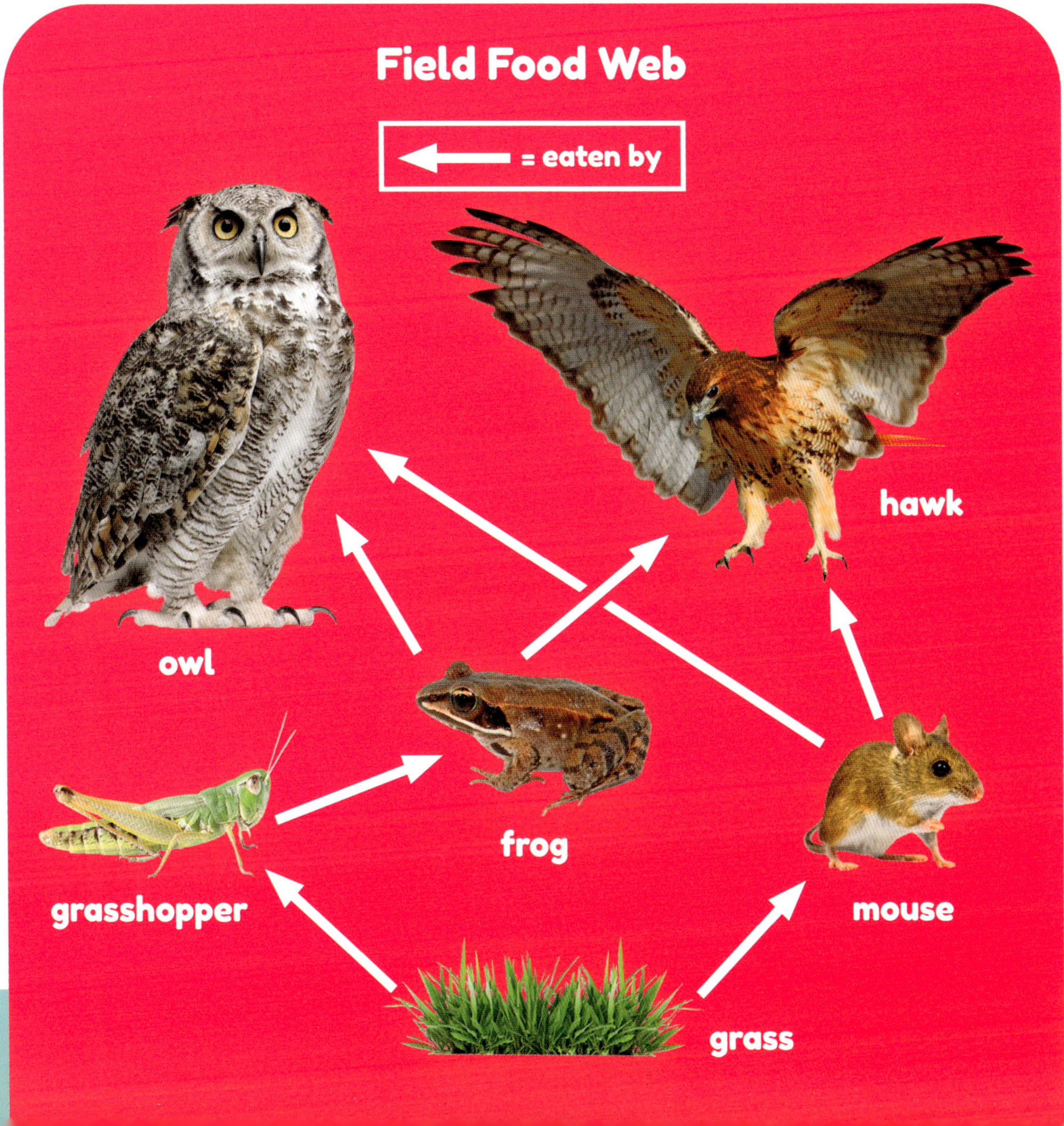

Hatching

All birds begin life inside an egg. When the baby bird is ready to emerge, it cracks the egg's shell open. Hatchlings are covered in soft down. They cannot fly or feed themselves. The baby birds stay in the nest. The parents protect and feed them.

Newborn birds must fully develop before they can live on their own.

FUN FACT!

Some birds have an egg tooth. They use this bony growth on their beaks to crack the eggshell.

A first flight brings a young bird closer to independence.

Chicks and Fledglings

As chicks, young birds begin to grow feathers. They need feathers to fly. Once a bird has its flight feathers, it takes its first flight. It is then called a fledgling.

Mature Adults

Adult birds are ready to find mates and build nests. Females lay eggs in nests. Most birds sit on their eggs to keep them warm. Then the life cycle begins again.

Seagull Life Cycle

Seagulls in the wild can live for 20 years or more.

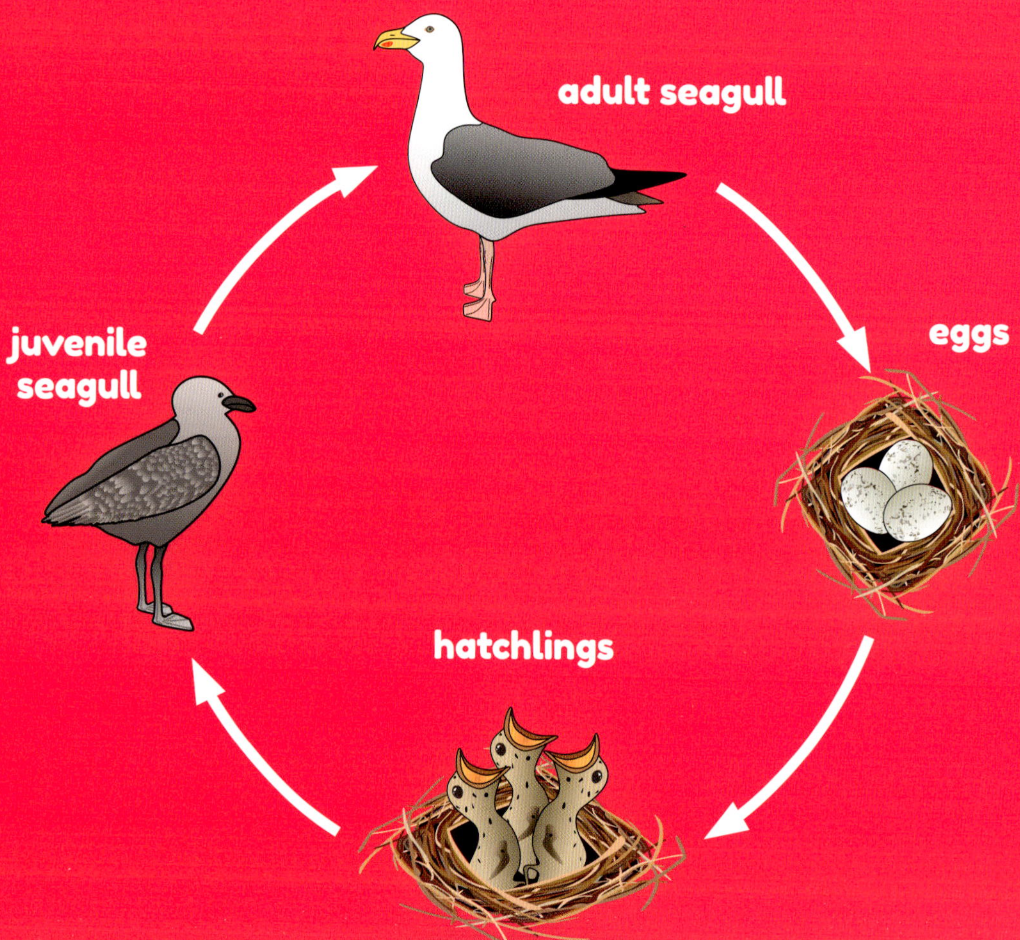

Like many other birds, hens on farms sit on eggs as the eggs develop.

Iguanas are large lizards that live in North America and South America.

The World of Reptiles

Reptiles are covered in scales, bony plates, or both. They are vertebrates. Snakes, turtles, lizards, and crocodiles are all reptiles. Except for snakes, most reptiles have four limbs.

Scaly Skin

Reptiles have dry skin covered with scales made of keratin. Scales protect reptiles from predators. Snakes have long scales on their bellies to help them move. Alligators have sharp, pointy scales.

Turtle shells are made of bony plates. Most reptiles shed their scaly skin regularly. They replace their scales with new ones.

Turtles are known for their bony, protective shells.

Reptiles, such as alligators, bask in the sun to stay warm.

Cold-Blooded

Reptiles are cold-blooded animals. They move to warmer or colder places when needed. Lizards sit in the sun to warm their bodies. Most reptiles become inactive during the winter.

Where Reptiles Live

Reptiles live almost everywhere except for extremely cold places. Many reptiles live in hot, humid areas. Snakes and lizards live on land, in trees, underground, or in water. Turtles live both on land and in the water. Alligators and crocodiles mainly live in the water. But they also spend some time on land.

Sea turtles swim through most of the world's oceans except for the polar regions.

What Reptiles Eat

A few reptiles, such as tortoises, eat only plants. Most reptiles eat other animals. They eat insects, birds, mice, frogs, and fish. Some chase their prey. Others hide and wait for prey to come close.

Chameleons use their tongues to grab insects.

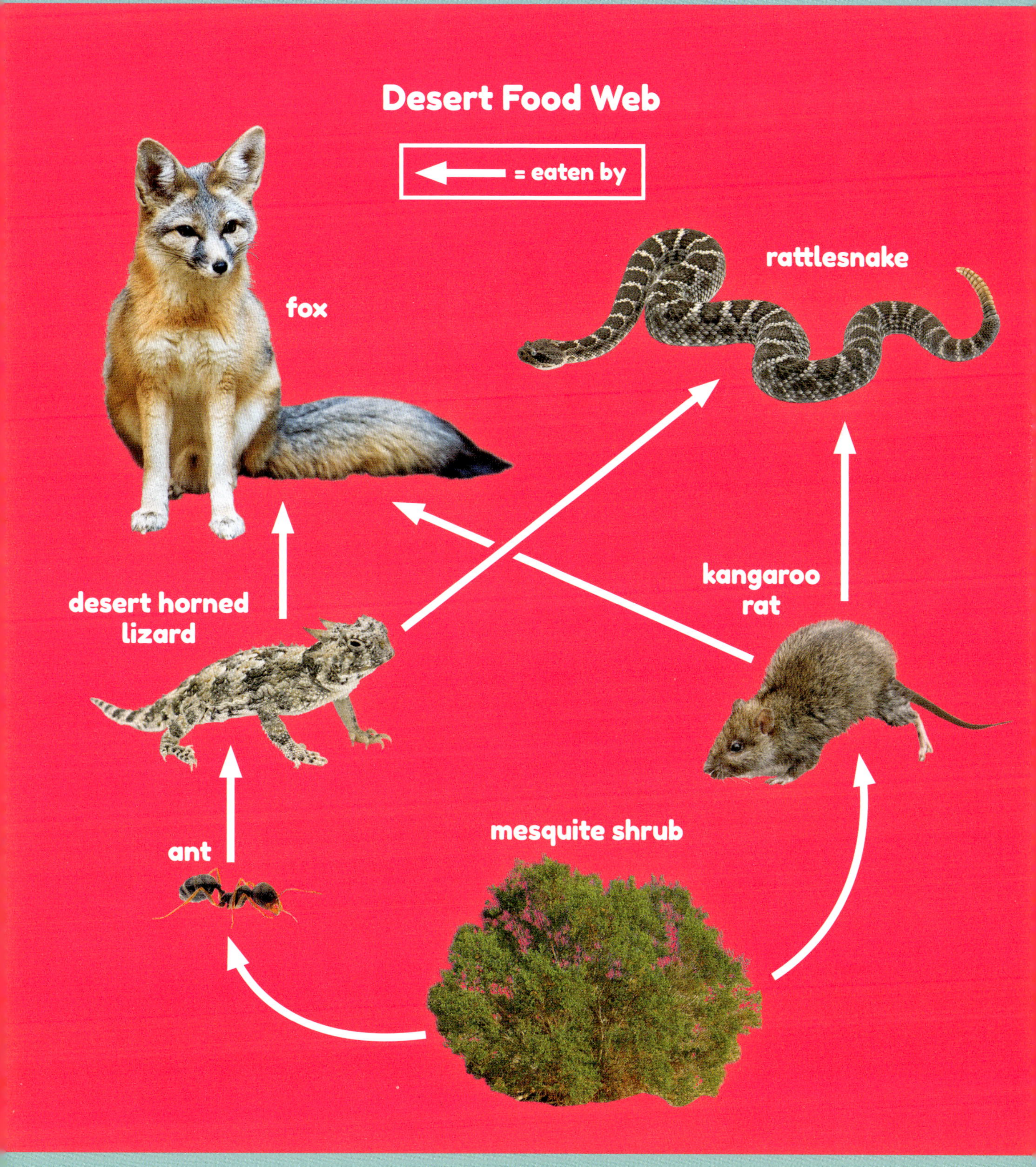
Desert Food Web
= eaten by
fox
rattlesnake
kangaroo
rat
desert horned
lizard
ant
mesquite shrub

It takes about 60 days before the eggs of the corn snake hatch.

Laying Eggs

Most reptiles lay eggs. Some lay only one or two. Others lay 100 or more. Reptiles lay eggs in different places. Geckos lay eggs beneath loose tree bark. Turtles dig egg chambers. After laying eggs, female turtles leave them. The eggs must survive alone.

Protecting the Eggs

A few reptile species stay with their eggs. Female crocodiles build nests out of soil and vegetation. They dig a hole in the nest and lay the eggs. They stay nearby to watch over the eggs. As the eggs hatch, mother crocodiles carry the babies to the water. They stay with their young for several months.

Live Young

Some snakes do not lay eggs. Boa constrictors and vipers give birth to live young.

Nile crocodiles may carry their young in their mouths.

Growing into Adults

Young reptiles usually look like small adults. These juveniles grow for a year or more before becoming adults. Adult reptiles find mates and produce young.

FUN FACT!

A tortoise named Jonathan turned 190 years old in 2022.

A Long Life

Reptiles can live for many years. Some large snakes and lizards can live more than 20 years. Sea turtles may live more than 50 years.

The desert lizards known as Gila monsters become adults by age five.

Snake Life Cycle

Larger reptiles generally have longer life spans.

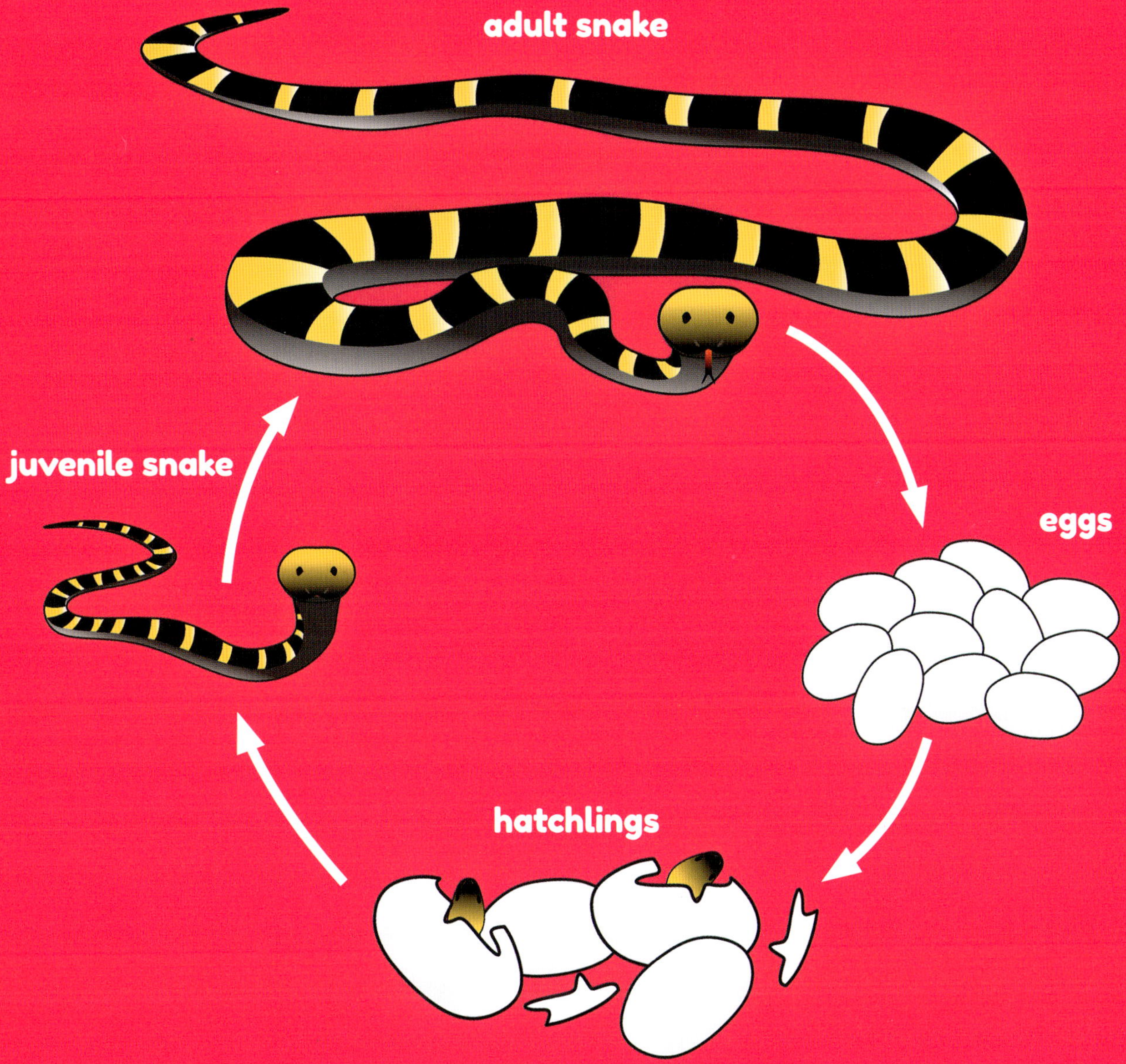

Frogs use their large, powerful back legs for jumping.

All about Amphibians

Amphibians can live on land or in the water. They are vertebrates. Frogs, toads, salamanders, and newts are all amphibians.

Hibernation

Many amphibians hibernate during winter months. They slow their heartbeats to survive.

Cold-Blooded

Amphibians are cold-blooded. They warm themselves in the sun. If they get too hot, amphibians move into the shade.

The Chinese fire-bellied newt can swim through the water.

Slimy Skin

Most amphibians have slimy skin. Mucus keeps their skin moist. Amphibians can absorb oxygen through their skin. If their skin gets too dry, amphibians will die. Many amphibians also have lungs. Some use gills to breathe.

Amphibians must stay moist to survive.

Some amphibians, including the fire salamander, contain toxins that make them dangerous to predators.

FUN FACT!

Amphibian comes from a Greek word meaning "double life."

Water and Land

Many amphibians live in hot, humid places. Habitats that are too sunny can dry out their skin. Amphibians usually live partly in water and partly on land.

Poison Defense

Many amphibians have poisons in their bodies. These poisons harm predators that try to eat them. Poisonous amphibians are often brightly colored. These bright colors warn predators to stay away.

Frogs eat insects, including butterflies.

Finding Food

Amphibians eat a variety of foods. Frogs, toads, and salamanders eat small animals such as insects, spiders, and worms. Larger amphibians may eat small birds and mammals.

Catching Prey

Many amphibians use their sharp eyesight to catch prey. Frogs and toads wait for prey to come nearby. Then they grab it with their mouths.

They catch prey such as flies by flicking their tongues. Salamanders grab prey with their strong jaws. Adult amphibians do not chew their food. Instead, they swallow it whole.

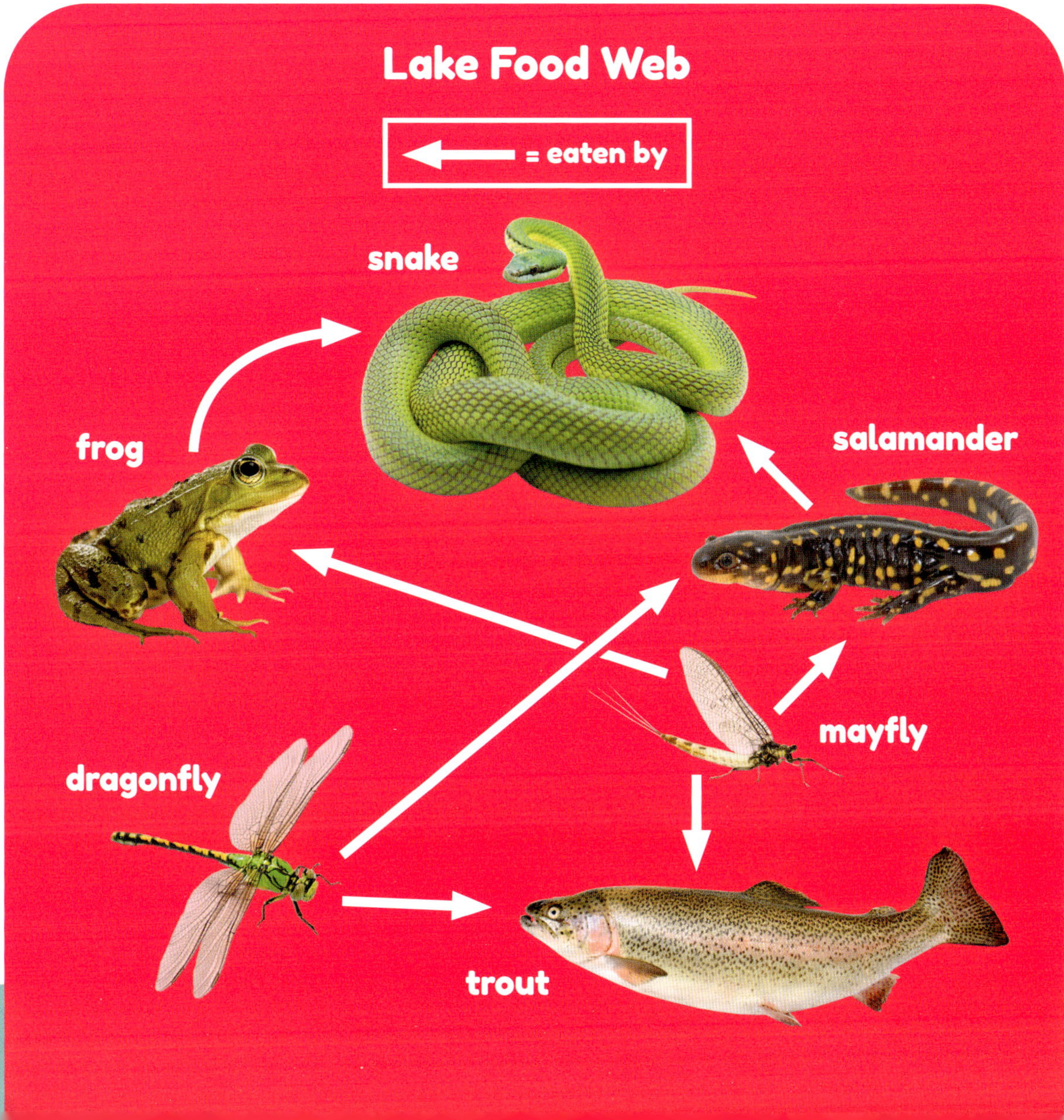

Reticulated glass frogs lay their eggs on leaves.

Many Eggs

Most amphibians lay eggs in water or in a wet, protected place. A few amphibian species give birth to live young. Amphibian eggs do not have shells. They have little protection from predators. Amphibians lay thousands of eggs to increase the chances of some surviving. Most eggs hatch within a few weeks.

Larvae

Amphibians hatch from eggs as larvae. Larvae look much different from adults. The larvae have gills to breathe underwater. The larval stage can last for weeks, months, or even years. The length depends on the species. A few amphibian species do not hatch as larvae. Instead, they look like miniature adults.

A toad larva, known as a tadpole, looks much different from the amphibian's adult form.

Metamorphosis

The larva undergoes metamorphosis and develops into an adult. Metamorphosis is a series of changes in an animal's body. During metamorphosis, the larva loses its gills and develops lungs. Lungs allow it to breathe on land. The amphibian's body also changes. It may grow legs or lose a tail.

Chinese giant salamanders can grow to 5.9 feet (1.8 m) long. They are the biggest amphibians in the world.

Amphibian Life Cycle

Frogs go through major changes in their life cycles.

There are more than 100,000 species of flies.

Millions of Insects

Insects are the largest group of animals on Earth. Scientists have discovered more than one million insect species. They believe there are millions more. Butterflies, ants, flies, grasshoppers, and bees are insects.

Exoskeletons

Insects are invertebrates. They do not have skeletons inside their bodies. Instead, they have hard exoskeletons that cover their bodies.

FUN FACT!

Insects are part of a larger group called arthropods. Spiders, ticks, lobsters, and crabs are also arthropods.

The exoskeleton provides protection. It can be stiff or flexible. The exoskeleton can be heavy. Or it can be light enough for an insect to be able to fly. Some exoskeletons are waterproof.

Flies have compound eyes made of many small parts.

Segmented Body

An insect's body is divided into three sections, called segments. The head holds the insect's antennae, eyes, and mouthparts. The middle segment is the thorax. An insect's six legs attach to its thorax. Some insects have wings attached to the thorax.

Abdomen

The end segment is the abdomen. The abdomen can be divided into multiple parts. Organs for digestion and reproduction are in the abdomen.

Ants have clearly separated body segments.

Sensing the Environment

Insects use their antennae and legs to sense their surroundings. Their legs and antennae can feel vibrations and movement. Insects also use antennae to smell. Some insects can taste with their feet.

Insects Everywhere

Insects live almost everywhere on Earth. Some crickets live in snowy regions. Some beetles and cockroaches live in hot deserts. Many insects burrow into the ground to survive harsh conditions.

Butterflies use their feet to taste things.

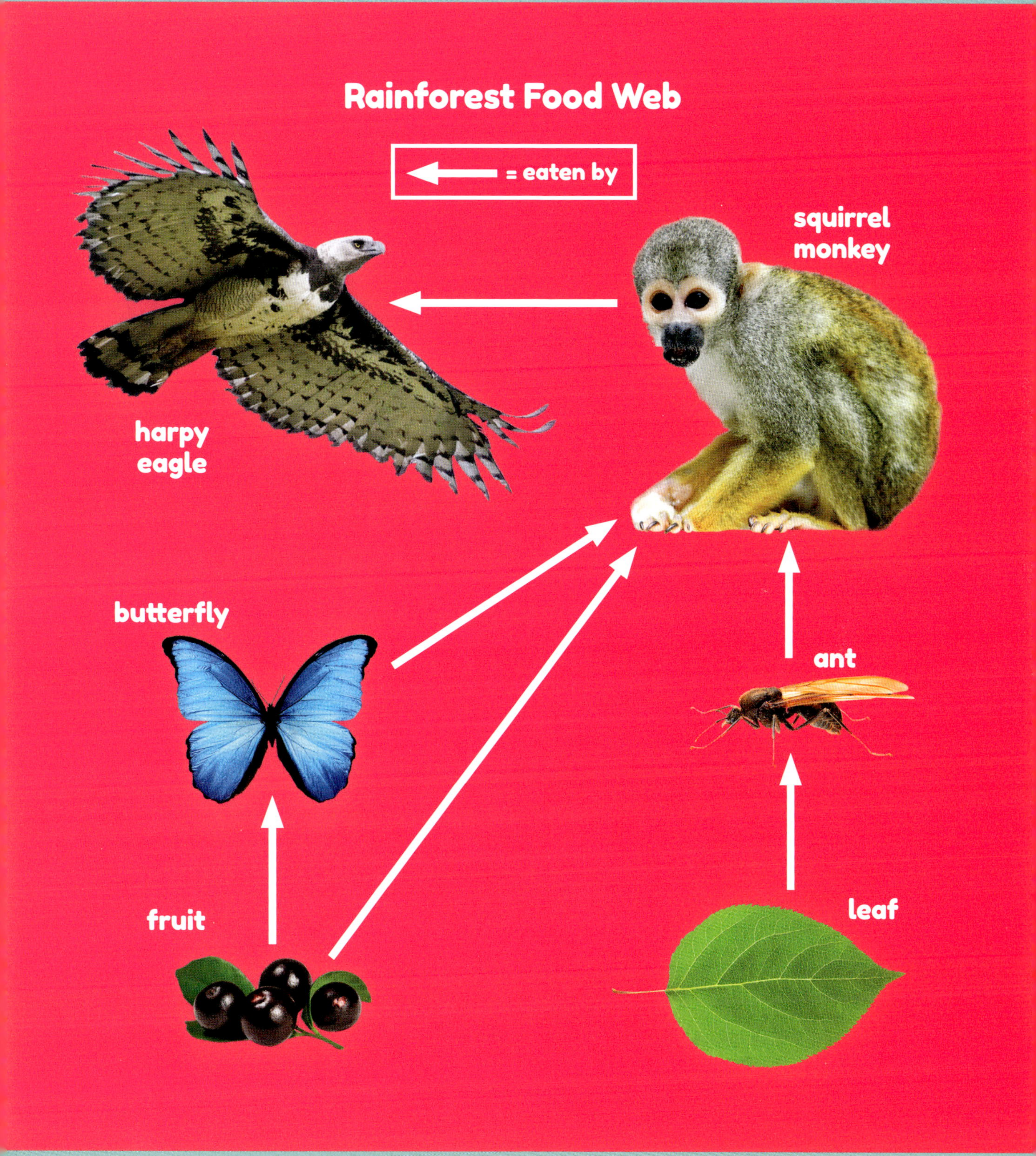
Rainforest Food Web
= eaten by
squirrel monkey
harpy eagle
butterfly
ant
fruit
leaf

Insects may lay their eggs on plant stems.

Life Begins with an Egg

Most insects start life as an egg. A few types are born live. Insects have two main life cycles. One is molting. The other is metamorphosis.

Molting

Some insects hatch from eggs and look like tiny adults. They include grasshoppers and cockroaches. As they grow, their exoskeletons become too small. The insects molt. This means they shed their old exoskeletons. They develop new, larger exoskeletons. The insects grow and molt until they become full-size adults.

Metamorphosis

Other insects undergo metamorphosis. Insects such as butterflies and moths go through four main stages in this life cycle. These stages are egg, larva, pupa, and adult.

A cicada emerges from its old exoskeleton in the process of molting.

Caterpillars eat leaves as they develop and grow.

From Egg to Butterfly

A butterfly begins life as an egg. It hatches as a larva. A butterfly larva is called a caterpillar. The larva eats, grows, and molts. Once it has grown enough, the caterpillar creates a protective shell called a chrysalis.

Transformation

The growing butterfly is then called a pupa. Inside the chrysalis, the pupa transforms. It develops wings, legs, and eyes. The pupa emerges from the chrysalis as an adult butterfly. It then flies away to find food and a mate.

Butterfly Life Cycle

In most butterfly species, adults live only a few weeks.

Pine trees are found in many areas of the Northern Hemisphere.

Plants around the World

Plants live anywhere there is sunlight, air, and soil. Mosses grow in Antarctica. Giant water lilies sprout in tropical rainforests. Tall pine trees thrive on mountains. And many cacti and shrubs grow well in hot deserts.

FUN FACT!

A botanist is a scientist who studies plants.

The stiff structure of bamboo is made mostly of cellulose.

Common Characteristics

Plants use sunshine, air, and water to make their food. Unlike animals, plants do not move. They are rooted in one place. Their cells have stiff walls made from a material called cellulose. Cellulose makes tree trunks and branches rigid.

Multicellular Plants

Plants are multicellular. Plant cells group together to form tissues. The parts of plants are made up of tissues. Plant parts include leaves, stems, roots, flowers, fruits, and seeds.

A plant's fruit helps protect its seeds.

Parts of a Plant

Each plant part has a specific function.

The shape of a plant's leaf is suited to the environment in which it lives.

Leaves

Plant leaves can be different sizes, shapes, and textures. The surface of a leaf has tiny holes called stomata. Stomata are usually on the underside of the leaf.

Exchange of Gases

The stomata open for the plant to exchange gases. The plant takes in carbon dioxide from the air. It releases oxygen and water vapor.

FUN FACT!

Plants that live in the desert store water in their leaves.

A leaf's stomata can be clearly seen under a microscope.

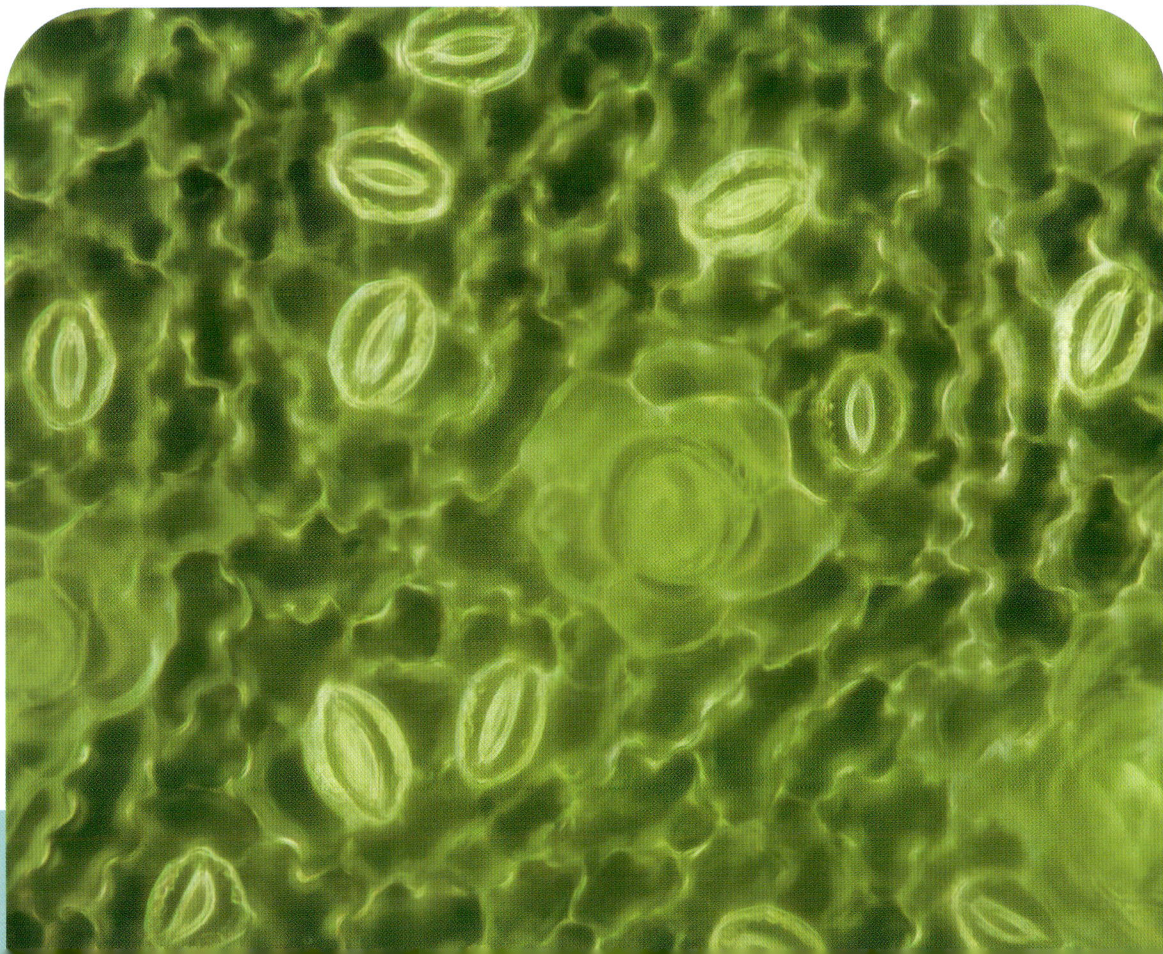

Sunshine helps crops around the world grow.

Turning Sunlight into Food

Leaves turn sunlight into food. Chlorophyll is the material that makes leaves green. It absorbs energy from sunlight. The plant uses this energy to power a chemical reaction. It takes in carbon dioxide and water. It creates oxygen and a sugar called glucose. Glucose gives the plant energy to live and grow. This process is called photosynthesis.

Photosynthesis

Photosynthesis is a key process for life on Earth.

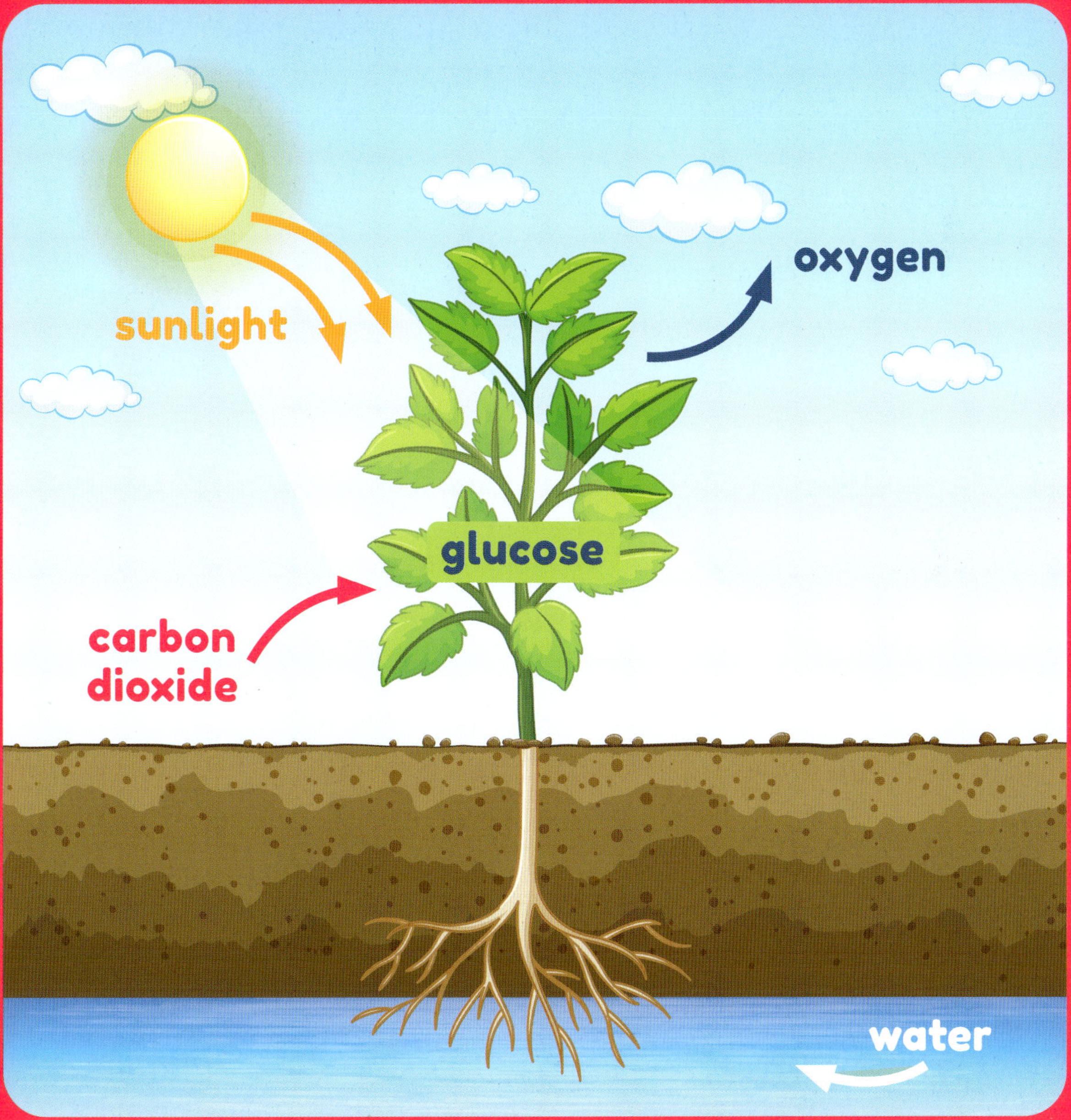

Stems

A plant's stem holds it upright. The stem supports branches, flowers, and fruit. It carries water and nutrients from the roots to the leaves. The stem also delivers glucose from the leaves to the rest of the plant.

Protection

Bark protects some plant stems from damage caused by animals. Bark also protects a plant's stem from hot or cold temperatures. For example, bark insulates maple trees during cold winters. It keeps the tree's trunk warm so the water inside the tree does not freeze.

The stems of some plants, including roses, have thorns on them.

There are more than 100 species of maple trees.

Roots

Roots anchor a plant in place. Most roots grow in the soil. But some plants have roots that float in water or wrap around branches.

Roots can extend deep into the ground even for small plants.

Taking Up Water and Nutrients

Roots absorb water, minerals, and nutrients from the soil. Some plants have a single deep root. Other plants have a network of many roots. Water, minerals, and nutrients travel from the roots into the stem. From there, they reach the rest of the plant.

Farmers grow carrots that have large, tasty roots.

Storage System

Roots store nutrients and water. The plant uses these stored nutrients and water when needed. Sometimes people eat plant roots. Carrots and sweet potatoes are root vegetables that many people enjoy.

Transpiration

Sometimes plants absorb more water than they need. Extra water leaves the plant through a process called transpiration. Water travels from the plant's roots to its leaves. Then the water evaporates. The plant releases it through the open stomata.

Plants that receive too much water use transpiration to balance their water levels.

People plant seeds on farms and in gardens around the world.

Plant Life Cycle

A seed is the part of a plant that can grow into a new plant. Most plants begin life as a seed. A seed can enter the soil in several ways. It can be carried by water, wind, or animals. Sometimes people plant seeds too.

Spreading Seeds

Some seeds fall to the ground. Wind and water can spread seeds far away. Wind carries dandelion seeds as far as 500 miles (800 km).

Dandelion seeds have adapted to be easily spread by wind.

Animals Carry Seeds

Animals also spread seeds. Squirrels collect and hide nuts from oak trees. Many of these hidden nuts become new trees.

The nut-gathering behavior of squirrels helps spread seeds.

Seeds in Animal Waste

Some animals spread seeds in their waste. Animals such as badgers eat fruit with seeds. The seeds pass through their bodies into their waste. This spreads the seeds to new places.

Seed Germination

A new plant begins to grow when the seed germinates. The roots and leaves sprout from the seed. A young plant that first appears above the soil is called a seedling.

Seedlings Grow

The seedling grows until it becomes a mature plant. As it grows, the plant needs sunlight, air, and water. It needs nutrient-rich soil. And it needs enough space from other plants. As the plant grows, its roots get stronger. More leaves and branches emerge.

Having more leaves allows a plant to capture more energy from the sun.

Pollination

A mature plant is ready to grow flowers. In most plants, a flower has both male and female parts. The male part is called a stamen. The female part is called a pistil. The stamen produces a powdery substance called pollen. Pollination is the process of moving pollen from one plant's stamen to another plant's pistil.

How Pollen Spreads

Pollen is often spread by insects. Insects sit on flowers to sip a sweet fluid called nectar. Pollen sticks to the insects as they fly from plant to plant. Sometimes, the wind carries pollen to the pistils. Fertilization takes place after pollination. In this process, the plant produces fruit or seeds.

The Pollination Process

Bees commonly act as pollinators.

Spores Create New Plants

Not all plants grow from seeds. Plants such as ferns and mosses grow from spores. The plant releases spores. The wind carries the spores to new areas. If the spore lands in a place where the conditions are right, it grows into a plant.

Spores rise from moss, allowing the moss to reproduce.

New Plants from Old Plants

Some plants grow from a piece of another plant. This process is called vegetative propagation. Potatoes, for example, grow from tubers. These are parts of the plant's roots. Garlic and onion plants grow from bulbs. Strawberry plants spread with stolons. These look like branches growing on the ground. The stolons develop roots and grow into new strawberry plants.

Cows graze on large fields of plant life.

Plants as Producers

Plants have an important role in ecosystems. They are producers. This means they make their own food. They use photosynthesis to do this.

Eating Plants

Insects, birds, and other animals eat plants. The energy in the plants moves into the animals. Larger animals eat the plant-eating animals. The energy moves again from one animal to another.

When people eat beef hamburgers, they are taking in energy that was originally in the plants that cows ate.

Plants as Shelter

Plants provide shelter for many animals. Shelters protect animals from predators. They are also places for animals to sleep, eat, and raise young.

Animals such as owls nest in trees for safety.

Even some of the world's largest animals can use a tree's shade to cool off.

Tree House

One tree can provide shelter for many animals. A caterpillar finds shelter under a leaf. A bird nests high in the tree's branches. Ants and other insects live on the tree trunk. Larger mammals use the tree for shade.

Classifying Plants

Scientists classify plants based on similarities and differences. Plants are divided into two main groups. The first group produces seeds. New plants grow from the seeds. The second group does not produce seeds. These plants reproduce in other ways.

Ferns are not seed-bearing plants.

The sunflower is an example of a seed-bearing plant.

Producing Seeds

Many plants produce seeds. This is how they reproduce. A seed holds a tiny plant embryo inside a hard seed coat.

Parts of a Seed

The seed coat protects a plant embryo from damage.

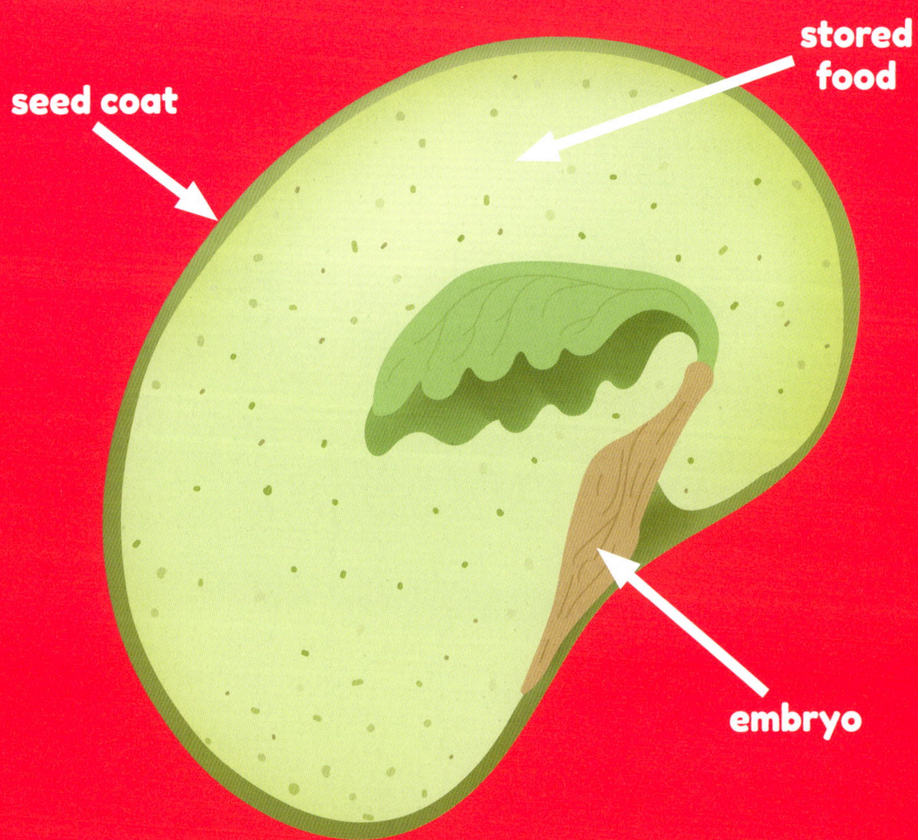

Nutritional Seeds

A seed also contains nutrients for the plant embryo. The nutrients provide food that the new plant needs to grow. Seeds can sit inactive in the soil for years until growing conditions are right. Seeds need warmth, water, and air to start growing.

What Is a Plant Embryo?

A plant embryo holds early forms of a plant's roots, stem, and leaves.

Plant seeds come in many shapes and sizes.

A Variety of Seeds and Plants

Many different types of seed-bearing plants grow around the world. Some are tall with needle-like leaves. These include pine trees. Others are smaller and have beautiful flowers. They include rose bushes. Some plants make many seeds. Others make only a few. Some seeds are hard and small, while others are large.

Redwoods, the world's tallest trees, are seed-bearing plants.

There are more than 300,000 kinds of flowering plants.

SEED-BEARING PLANTS

Powerful microscopes reveal the channels that run through plant tissue.

Phloem is found in the outer rings of a tree trunk. Xylem is closer to the trunk's center.

Vascular Plants

All seed-bearing plants are vascular. This means they have tissues that move water and nutrients. A tissue called phloem carries food away from the leaves. A tissue called xylem moves water and nutrients from the roots to the rest of the plant.

Trees such as maples have winged helicopter seeds.

Fertilization

Seed-bearing plants have flowers or cones. In these places, pollen from male plant parts makes contact with female plant parts. After pollination, fertilization occurs. A tiny plant embryo then forms inside the seed.

Seeds Scatter

Seeds scatter in many ways. Animals, wind, or water carry seeds away from their parent plants. Some plants make seeds in a pod. As the seeds grow, the pod swells. When it bursts, seeds shoot out like tiny missiles.

Plant Life Cycle

Farmers carefully watch the life cycle of a plant when growing food.

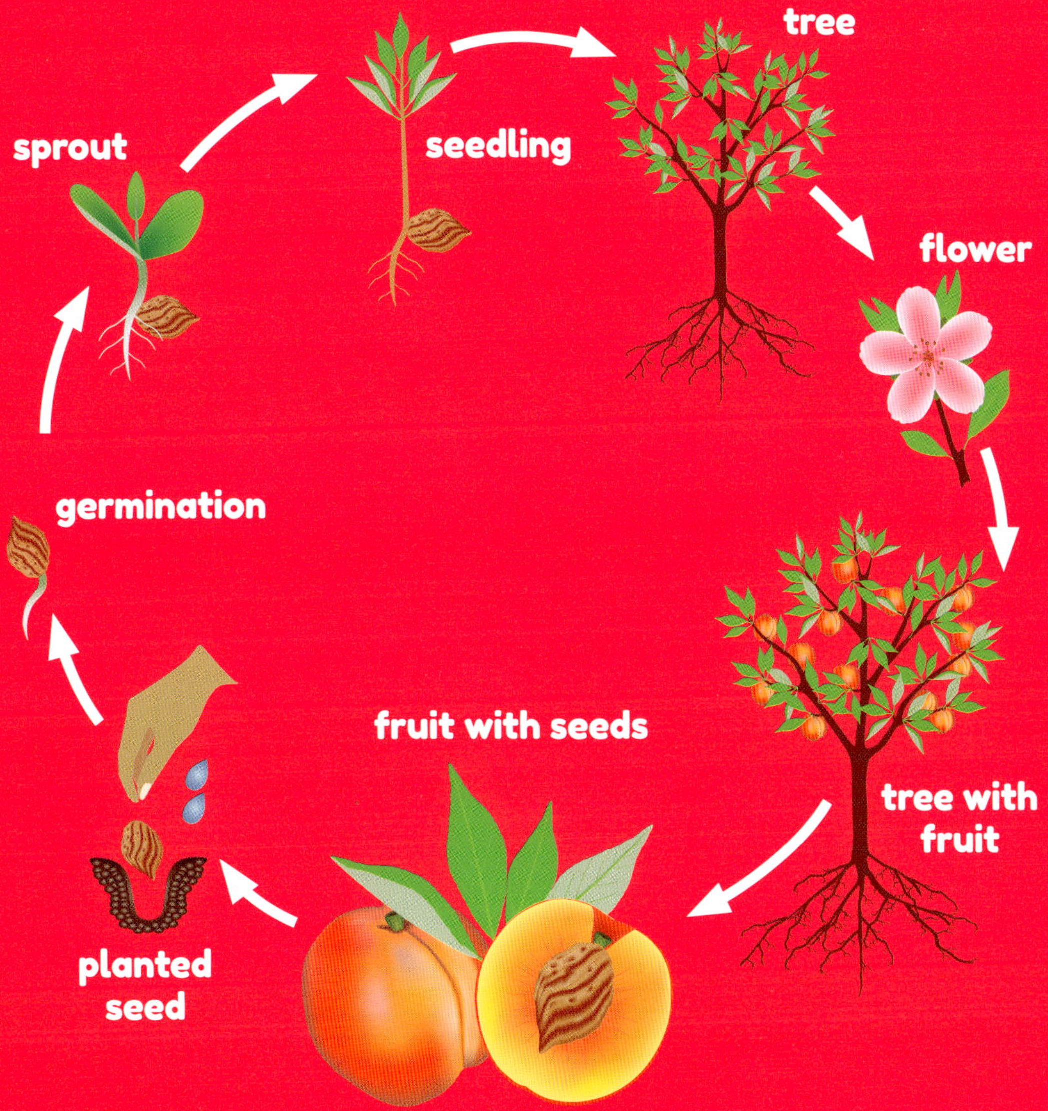

Gymnosperms

Seed-bearing plants belong to one of two main groups. These are gymnosperms and angiosperms. Gymnosperms are plants with cones. These plants do not have flowers or fruit. Instead, their seeds are held inside cones.

A single tree can grow a large number of cones.

Unlike other kinds of trees, evergreens do not lose their leaves in winter.

Trees with Cones

Evergreen trees, such as pines, are gymnosperms. These trees have needle-like leaves that stay green year-round. They surround their seeds in cones. Other common gymnosperms include cedar, juniper, redwood, and spruce trees.

Apple trees, which are angiosperms, are grown on farms called orchards.

Angiosperms

Like gymnosperms, angiosperms produce seeds. However, angiosperms also produce flowers and fruit. Angiosperms are a very diverse group. Many plants grown for food are angiosperms.

Fruit Trees

Cherry, apple, and pear trees are angiosperms. Flowering azalea shrubs are angiosperms too. Many vegetables and grains are angiosperms. These include carrots, peas, and oats.

Farmers produce millions of tons of oats each year.

No Seeds

Seedless plants have leaves, stems, and roots like other plants. But they do not have seeds. That means they do not produce flowers or fruits. Ferns, mosses, liverworts, and horsetails are all seedless plants. Many grow in swamps, in forests, and on tree trunks.

Moss can be found growing on rocks and logs.

Horsetails date back millions of years to the age of the dinosaurs.

Spores

Many seedless plants produce spores instead of seeds. A spore is a single cell. Unlike a seed, a spore does not have stored food for a new plant.

Spores Spread

Seedless plants release thousands of spores. The spores are very light. Wind and water spread them to new areas. Many seedless plants grow in damp or shady areas. They need a lot of moisture to grow and reproduce.

Shady forest floors are an ideal place for moss to grow.

Fragmentation

Some seedless plants reproduce through fragmentation. A small piece, or fragment, of the plant breaks off and falls to the ground. That piece can grow and become a new plant. Hornworts and liverworts reproduce using fragmentation.

Hornwort is an aquatic plant often used in aquariums.

A small piece of liverwort can continue growing after being separated from its original plant.

Ferns are often found in forests.

Ferns

Ferns are a type of seedless plant. Ferns have roots and stems. They have large leaves called fronds. Thousands of types of ferns grow on Earth. Some can grow more than 65 feet (20 m) tall. Some carry their spores on tall stalks. Others store their spores along their stems or under their leaves.

Seedless Vascular Plants

Ferns are vascular plants. They have tissue that moves water and nutrients throughout the plant. Horsetails and clubmosses are also seedless vascular plants.

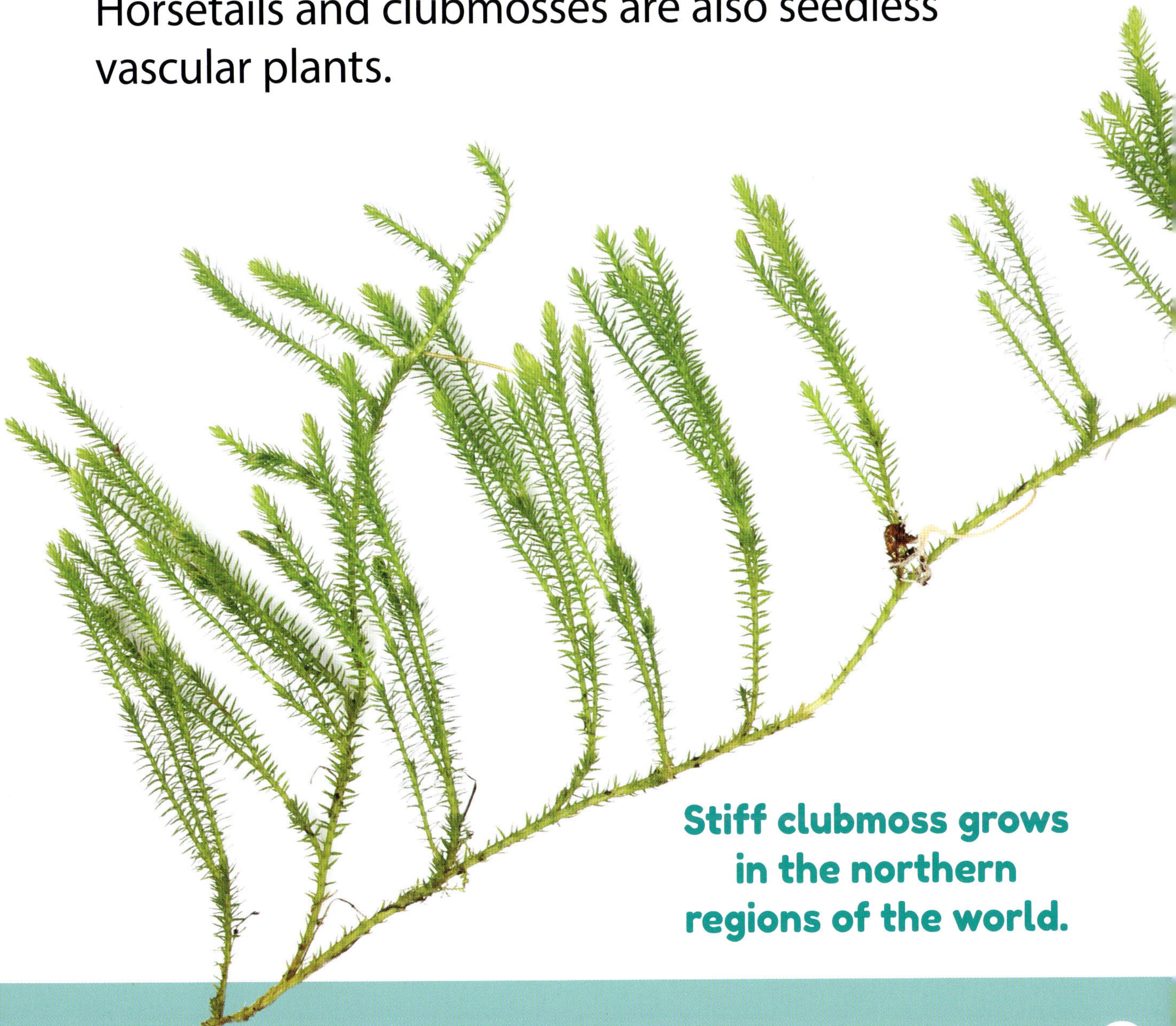

Stiff clubmoss grows in the northern regions of the world.

A close-up view of a growing fern shows the rhizoids that connect it to the surface below.

Bryophytes

Bryophytes are a group of seedless plants. They include mosses, liverworts, and hornworts. Bryophytes do not have true roots, stems, or leaves. Instead, they have small hair-like structures called rhizoids. They use rhizoids to anchor themselves to a surface.

Nonvascular Plants

Bryophytes are nonvascular plants. They do not have an internal system to carry water. This means they need to be in or near water to thrive.

Bryophytes need a source of moisture to survive.

Mosses

Mosses are soft and spongy seedless plants. They grow up to only a few inches tall. Mosses do not have roots or stems. Rhizoids anchor them to rocks and soil. Mosses take in water and nutrients through green leaf-like parts.

FUN FACT!

Liverworts are believed to be one of the first plants that grew on Earth.

Mosses can be grown on indoor walls for decoration.

Structures called spore capsules hold a moss plant's spores.

Mosses Produce Spores

Like ferns, mosses produce spores. The wind carries the spores away from the parent plant. If conditions are good, each spore can grow into a new moss plant. They usually grow in damp and shady places.

Liverworts

Liverworts are small, flat plants that grow along the ground. They do not have roots. Instead, liverworts absorb moisture through their rhizoids.

GLOSSARY

classify
To sort things into groups according to their characteristics.

ecosystem
A community of animals and plants interacting with their environment.

embryo
The earliest stage in the development of a fertilized egg.

fertilize
To begin reproduction in an egg or a plant.

gestation
The period when an embryo develops inside its mother.

invertebrate
An animal that does not have a backbone.

larva
The early form of an animal, such as an insect, after it hatches from an egg.

mucus
A slimy fluid.

pollination
The process of transferring pollen between flowers for reproduction.

predator
An animal that hunts and eats other animals.

prey
An animal that is hunted and eaten by other animals.

species
A group of animals or plants that share characteristics and can mate and produce offspring.

vertebrate
An animal that has a backbone.

TO LEARN MORE

More Books to Read

Hoare, Ben. *The Secret World of Plants*. DK, 2022.

Life Cycles: Everything from Start to Finish. DK, 2020.

Spelman, Lucy H. *Animal Encyclopedia: 2,500 Animals with Photos, Maps, and More!* National Geographic, 2021.

Online Resources

Booklinks
NONFICTION NETWORK
FREE! ONLINE NONFICTION RESOURCES

To learn more about life science, please visit **abdobooklinks.com** or scan this QR code. These links are routinely monitored and updated to provide the most current information available.

INDEX

PHOTO CREDITS

Cover Photos: Shutterstock Images, front (bee, chick and egg, grass, hen, sunflower); Alexander Raths/ Shutterstock Images, back

Interior Photos: Sari O'Neal/Shutterstock Images, 1; Aleksey Zhuravlev/Shutterstock Images, 3; Volodymyr Burdiak/Shutterstock Images, 4; Rainer von Brandis/E+/Getty Images, 5; Shutterstock Images, 6 (ant), 6 (cell), 8, 9, 10, 15 (shrub), 15 (mountain lion), 15 (nuts), 16, 17 (kangaroo), 19 (life cycle), 20, 21, 22 (top), 22 (fish icon), 24, 25 (tuna), 25 (plankton), 25 (sea star), 25 (shark), 25 (seagull), 26 (bottom), 26 (fish icon), 28 (fish icon), 30 (bird icon), 37 (grasshopper), 37 (hawk), 38, 40, 41, 47 (rat), 47 (lizard), 49 (snake), 49 (bottom), 50, 51, 52 (top), 52 (frog icon), 53, 55 (frog), 56, 62, 64, 65, 67 (butterfly), 67 (fruit), 67 (leaf), 70, 71, 72, 76, 79, 80, 82, 83, 84, 86, 90, 94, 100, 101, 102, 103 (plant), 104, 105, 108, 114, 114–115, 116, 119, 120, 121, 124, 125 (plant icon); Bryan Faust/Shutterstock Images, 7; Eric Isselee/Shutterstock Images, 11, 13, 15 (deer), 35, 37 (owl), 57 (mayfly), 57 (frog); Budimir Jevtic/Shutterstock Images, 12; Dongyang Zhang/Shutterstock Images, 14; Pranee Jirakitdachakun/Shutterstock Images, 15 (grass), 37 (grass); Irina K./Shutterstock Images, 15 (squirrel); Olha Semeniv/Shutterstock Images, 17 (bottom); Mogens Trolle/Shutterstock Images, 18; Tom Fricker Design/Shutterstock Images, 19 (whale); Dennis Forster/Shutterstock Images, 23; Jiang Hongyan/ Shutterstock Images, 25 (mussels); Zykov Vladimir/Shutterstock Images, 27; Peter Leahy/Shutterstock Images, 28 (top); Kazakova Maryia/Shutterstock Images, 29, 61; Narupon Nimpaiboon/Shutterstock Images, 30 (top); Jesse Nguyen/Shutterstock Images, 31; Passakorn Umpornmaha/Shutterstock Images, 32; Natalia Golovina/Shutterstock Images, 32–33; Rob Jansen/Shutterstock Images, 34; Yongkiet Jitwattanatam/ Shutterstock Images, 36; Rudmer Zwerver/Shutterstock Images, 37 (mouse); Gerald A. DeBoer/Shutterstock Images, 37 (frog), 57 (salamander); Vishnevskiy Vasily/Shutterstock Images, 39; Erik Lam/Shutterstock Images, 42; Korkin Vadim/Shutterstock Images, 43; Nicole Kwiatkowski/Shutterstock Images, 44; Michael Smith ITWP/Shutterstock Images, 45; Lisdiyanto Suhardjo/Shutterstock Images, 46; Kevin Oke Photo/ Shutterstock Images, 47 (mesquite); Jay Pierstorff/Shutterstock Images, 47 (snake); Danut Vieru/Shutterstock Images, 47 (ant); Virrage Images/Shutterstock Images, 47 (fox); Dan Olsen/Shutterstock Images, 48; Rafael Silva/Shutterstock Images, 54; Petlin Dmitry/Shutterstock Images, 55 (top), 57 (snake); Alexander Raths/Shutterstock Images, 57 (trout); Hintau Aliaksei/Shutterstock Images, 57 (dragonfly); G. J. Verspui/ Shutterstock Images, 58; Matej Ziak/Shutterstock Images, 59; Tristan Tan/Shutterstock Images, 60; Kriachko Oleksii/Shutterstock Images, 63; Yosin Kogoya/Shutterstock Images, 66; Rosa Jay/Shutterstock Images, 67 (monkey); Nick Garbutt/NaturePL/Science Source, 67 (eagle); Joao P. Burini/MYN/Nature Picture Library/ Alamy, 67 (ant); Brett Hondow/Shutterstock Images, 68; Tacio Philip Sansonovski/Shutterstock Images, 69; Nataly Studio/Shutterstock Images, 73; Boida Anatolii/Shutterstock Images, 74; Teguh Mujiono/Shutterstock Images, 75; Cornel Constantin/Shutterstock Images, 77; Taras Vyshnya/Shutterstock Images, 78; Mircea Costina/Shutterstock Images, 81; Elena Zhi/Shutterstock Images, 85; Romolo Tavani/Shutterstock Images, 87; Crystal Bradwin/Shutterstock Images, 88; Viktor Loki/Shutterstock Images, 89; Gan Chaonan/Shutterstock Images, 91; Blue Ring Media/Shutterstock Images, 93; Volodymyr Nikitenko/Shutterstock Images, 95; Leonid Ikan/Shutterstock Images, 96; Toufic Araman/Shutterstock Images, 97; Chase D'Animulls/Shutterstock Images, 98; Beate Wolter/Shutterstock Images, 99; Maria Evseyeva/Shutterstock Images, 103 (bottom); Power and Syred/Science Source, 106; Merkushev Vasiliy/Shutterstock Images, 107; Havryliuk Kharzhevska/ Shutterstock Images, 109; Karavanov Lev/Shutterstock Images, 110; Lecia Michelle/Shutterstock Images, 111; Paul Hardwick Images/Shutterstock Images, 112; Ines Behrens-Kunkel/Shutterstock Images, 113; Magnus Binnerstam/Shutterstock Images, 117; Joan Carles Juarez/Shutterstock Images, 118; Biophoto Associates/ Science Source, 122; Guillermo Guerao Serra/Shutterstock Images, 123; Henri Koskinen/Shutterstock Images, 125 (top)